Palimpsest

Poems by Maxine Silverman

DOS MADRES

2014

DOS MADRES PRESS INC.

P.O.Box 294, Loveland, Ohio 45140
www.dosmadres.com   editor@dosmadres.com

Dos Madres is dedicated to the belief that the small press is essential to the vitality of contemporary literature as a carrier of the new voice, as well as the older, sometimes forgotten voices of the past. And in an ever more virtual world, to the creation of fine books pleasing to the eye and hand.

Dos Madres is named in honor of Vera Murphy and Libbie Hughes, the "Dos Madres" whose contributions have made this press possible.

Dos Madres Press, Inc. is an Ohio Not For Profit Corporation and a 501 (c) (3) qualified public charity. Contributions are tax deductible.

Executive Editor: Robert J. Murphy

Illustration & Book Design: Elizabeth H. Murphy
www.illusionstudios.net
Cover image: "Joplin 2, Latch", collage by Maxine Silverman
www.maxinegsilverman.com
Photo of cover collage: Myles Aronowitz
www.LushPhotography.com

Typset in Adobe Garamond Pro & Pushkin
ISBN 978-1-939929-23-5
Library of Congress Control Number: 2014955845

First Edition

for Helen Allen

always with me

"I wrote fast, to compress and catch a lesson
while I could still hear it, and not because
it had happened to *me*, so that *I* was recording it,
but because it was important to the whole study."
- M.F.K. Fisher, *Sister Age*

TABLE OF CONTENTS

Back at the Buena Vista

Body Braille

Palimpsest

Back at the Buena Vista

LA NATIVIDAD

Across from the mini mall where *los hombros* mill and wait
for contractors or landscapers to drive up and point *c'mon get in*,
where the lucky ones shoulder their way into a day's work,
and the others regroup, their breath rising with exhaust,
some of them hunker by the curb, some tug gray hoods over dark hair,
shrug or breathe into cupped palms and stamp,
none of them check the time,
across from that place

Our Lady of Perpetual Hope
towers above a toy village laid out on the Buena Vista's straggly strip of a yard.
Gazing at the small stable, miniscule crib lined with fresh straw,
her face serene, fluttering chipped hem, palm to palm between blue breasts,
she stands ready in the cold morning light to adore.
Around her a rejoicing host
of lawn sculptures, ceramic elf, bunny, three improbably yellow ducks,
spotted fawn, white bird and a rosy one in the attitude of prayer,

and it is good they wait,
forbearance their gift.

Mercy on them,
a thousand tender mercies this winter day

on one who gathered the creatures so, her willingness to attend
the heart of ceremony. For what other purpose, after all,
should a flamingo bend his graceful neck,
the woman content herself expectantly?

And on those other men, the unchosen,
who wait for the light, for their luck, who drift back across the road,
and pausing at the creche, cross themselves,

a thousand most tender mercies.

BODY LANGUAGE

"Good you don't know what's coming,
'd scare you to death," he said.
"Just as well you don't remember," she said,
meaning all she endured because of him.

He said/she said—the body pays no mind,
does what a body does, lays knowing by
in muscle and marrow, larder for leaner days,
serving the soul a tasty mess to make dark sense or light.

So if I tell childhood's largesse: early morning, swimming laps
upon laps, cool reverie of breathe-pull-glide,

> *Liberty Park Pool, late 50's,*
> *two young women, sleek swans skimming along*
> *some stroke of their own luminous invention,*
> *side by side, confiding, smiling, saving their hair do's*
> *for the drive-in movie,*

you will know that I, body, soul, breathed them in.
Later I learned glamour, amour,

but I knew, treading water as they glide by,
sultry even in the pool, alluring and beyond reach, they

are the prize and I will sink unless somehow
my arms and legs move that way below the surface.

To the blue cord roping off the deep end
I splashed, vowing to learn their smooth stroke. *This* I'd practice.
I, too, would assume the form of pure ease and nonchalance,

enviable, beyond harm.

TRELLIS

Fooled by rain cooling the day, moonflowers bloom
  among fuchsia morning glories, the ebb and flow
of flowers laps over, and time idles

If the morning is a scroll, the trellis is a woman caught gathering
  blossoms as she bends for just one more before she bends
to retrieve the door key hidden in a stone.

If the trellis is a fan held to the breast of the woman's house,
  bees stagger from her crimson-throated garden mumbling
their wild alchemy, dust the parchment gold.

  Sun glimmers through rice paper clouds.

If she fans the leaves of paper lined with tendrils of ink,
  pages of iris pulp, bound by flax,
if she breathes lightly unfurling those sheaves

  surely she will see her father again
turning to give her mother the first fruit of seven trees,
  two apples, Jonagold, and Red Delicious, one Damson
plum,

  and in an ivory case she would fold them,
    securing the pleated orchard with a tiny clasp,
  slipping all that fragrance in the sleeve of her light summer
robe.

  The trellis, each lime-green leaf a lantern hung on a peg by her
gate.

WALK

Remember how your legs moved,
your year-old legs, left foot pointing right tripping
her sister? How every cell cried out *push*,
push your own stroller, kitchen chairs, anything
to steady your willing unable body forward,
earning mock praise from Uncle Sol, "Piano Mover."
The name stuck until your foot straightened
perforce, you strode

into the future where you stand now
at the top of the drive, gauging distance,
easy rain glazing blacktop to glitter.
Giddy, your first time out, spine straightened,
fortified with enough metal to rouse
airport security,

pushing your *modus operandi* ahead of you,
a walker, wheels rolling,
the body leaning into a soft January afternoon
ordered to believe what the mind ordains: now
  walk, baby, walk.

BACK AT THE BUENA VISTA

In the narrow border between porch and parking lot, there is barely
   room for the hydrangea to loll against the iron handrail,
mounds of purple blooms a fertility goddess would swoon for, spilling
   onto the macadam, a rose trellis leans on the concrete porch,
and a swan planter wafts sweet starry phlox, as wings.

Undaunted, someone set a staggered row of corn, seven, eight, nine green
   festoons. Zinnias I understand, tomatoes, there is room for tomatoes
along these low stucco dwellings. What chance for a single row of corn,
   even with a guardian *señora* enthroned on the porch to watch who comes,
who goes, when my own father maintained six rows, six, for yield?

And sunflowers before they flower, their green rays spike from green
   center, green stalks. Now I see them for what they are becoming, today
as I drive by it becomes clear to me, slowly by, and she stares equably,
   not glaring 'long as my wheels keep rolling on the hot tarry lot. What more
than desire and memory—hand to mouth farms in far away valleys,

or scattered on burnt hillsides—do these fountains of maize spew?
   In each season at the Buena Vista, the *señora* and a feast day. Sure
enough across the street, there lounge the men, *los hombros* sweltering
   for this weather's work, and sure enough, in the mirror I see they cross
and stand by the throne for her blessing, her blessing and a little shade.

SLOW WATER   DEEP TIME

"Momma, I can hear time go by under water."

The way voices carry over water
and distances expand,
your tethers loosen, and you lose yourself
coming going up back, east becoming west
becoming east, without belief to suspend.

How voices shimmer over time   light refracts black lines

below glisten of water   reflects glancing light swimmers

lanes of darker sequins dancing din low dimmer voices

listen traces iridescent iris limbs limning luminous laps

refluent voices lapse over and over time swimming laps

prism limbs mindless lungs warm deep time slow water

"Yes, darling child, that is your pulse, your heart beating"

in a lane glimmering no wider than the strip of dirt where

Buena Vista residents grow corn and roses,
where Our Lady of Perpetual Hope sojourns.

JUNE AT THE BUENA VISTA

Where Our Lady of Perpetual Hope and a rejoicing host
  waited in the snow before a tiny straw-lined crib, ready and willing to adore—
roses! Higgledy piggledy rows of roses tumble up and down a fanning trellis,
  raving rambunctious red
angels flexing, rope-a-doping, aching to wrestle any fool daring to sleep
  on that straggly strip of a lawn this rosy day-breaking dawn.
Wait. The foolish reference is not to baby Jesus. I'm talking Jacob,
  an earlier Jew, on the lam from snatching his brother's birthright. Plus,
I'm mixing the dreams and verses, first the ladder then the match
  of the epoch—Jacob vs. the man-angel-messenger-of-god—and he rose
from his epic battle, staggering, shivering in the desert chill of almost morning
  to meet Esau, twin of bound-blind lineage, Esau the estranged
who, Jacob had reason to fear, might want revenge, quench his bloodthirst,

that man thing, because Jacob stole their father's firstborn blessing too.
  Is that why? What about Rebecca? Mother betrayed. Momma chose Jacob.
Momma loved him more. After all the years and talk talk talk,
  no matter wives, sons, and flocks, big brother is still sore. Blessings
mattered then, the act of speaking false or true, the fact of speech itself
  becoming utterance, becoming oath and covenant. Words could kill, and did,
no doll required. Only God knows how many mothers dance
  on a voodoo pin, God Only knows.

The swan, who dipped her head in devotion last Decembers, in June anchors
  the trellis, resembling a peacock with rose-colored specs, hoping Our Lady
will reappear. Lugging all these dreams through history makes a body
  so tired all you think of is sleep, roses becoming angels or the dream of angels.
Stop. June at the Buena Vista. The nose knows. A rose is a rose. No angel
  smells that sweet.

THEN

She was the one who taught me to call
     Daddy   at night,   my mother
with child again so soon after my birth,

but he didn't hear   evidently   she hauled herself
down the dark hall to the darker room
I did not share yet and I confused who was to mother
me and so, her story goes, when she came home
from Bothwell Memorial with a newer baby, knelt,
opened her arms wide,
I turned and stumbled into his embrace.

Even with a twisted foot I could swim.
Another lesson my father taught   could not walk, could not run, ok
then, swim.   He taught me how.   She thought, *In the water no one*
                              will see. Too bad her foot born too bad
Specialist consulted, *straighten   exercise   or else . . .*
"Or else" gave shame license.

Mother twisted that foot
which hurt her more than me
hold still
first thing before shoes, last before bed,
however many in between, so that when I could stand
we stood always toe to toe.

And if she had not   this much is true
if pity had filled her   my foot would have bound me
tight as any China girl's,

so she twisted that foot and she twisted that foot.
Otherwise
I would not have been able to walk
away from her
into the world   looking   all over for someone
who loved to hurt me for my own good
          (truth distilled
          until it is false)
tracking prints and traces of stain
          (newer truth, a few years
          down the road)
unsatisfactory   refractory
(evidence) after all, I can walk
          a little herky jerky okey dokey   hopalong
but walking and   this I remember as if *then* were *now*

hoping one day some day
would be the day
my foot would be straight
enough
when she held it
her mouth would not set that hard line
my foot hurt her so
her hand clenched so
my foot hurt.

An accident of birth, just as who your mother—
or your father—is a flukey dukey
something that happened a long time ago

before we knew my spine would curve away
from that other pain
until the bones required titanium rods
to maintain space for breath
   (truth pared
    to an image)
before I knew what happened
would always have happened
   (a certain
    kind of
    truth)
and even that
was then,
before I knew today would be *some day,*

I would be all right,

I would be swimming laps.

INSIDE THE BUENA VISTA

Looking out I see her looking in
every morning early. The children
just left for school, not them she's after,
to throw in her minivan and snatch away,
and she's old for Manuel, though with that one
who can ever tell.

Any day I expect her to stop, knock, claim
my swan or angel is hers, stolen last time
her leaves were raked.
                              So far she only
cruises by, not I think checking license plates,
not crossing herself for the Lady, and even
when I sit on the porch and stare at her
she stares at me as if the railing is a cage.
Does she think we're here for her pleasure?

Or she has piles of clothing in the back,
some with stains and tears, but clean, she
claims she's only wondering if someone
or someone we know could use the shirts,
still good, very good still, just outgrown, only
too good for Goodwill.

NACIMIENTOS

The joke's on me, the drive by *gringa*
on her way to swim.
At first I wondered what whimsical child
had assembled the melangerie,
no, I decided later, a woman
bringing everything she could bear—
swan planter, plaster bunnies, tiny Victorian shops,
an almost life size Madonna, her wholehearted
gift turning the toys sacred.

Next morning evergreen garlands loop and twine
the white scrolled iron railing, on each swag
a corsage of pine cones.

Gracias to the young man talking
outside the Buena Vista, and I nod
to the elder woman on the porch,
her reddish woven shawl
drawn close against the early morning chill.
Concerned, he is urging her back inside,
when their cousin Sofia comes with the car,
the young man assures her, he, Paco Manuel, will knock.
My unfettered fantasia envelops the statuary and follows
the family inside, to sort laundry, buy cough syrup,
to meet the school bus in the afternoon.

Next, pinwheels whirl above the manger,
their blue and silver wings a flock of stars.
Enthralled, one wise man waits
for the others to arrive.

~ ~

Nacimientos are not, I read, only self portraits, mere
individual longing, so much as cultural.
Lavish multi tiered panoramas furnish living rooms,
porches and sidewalks of certain *vecindarios,*

tin foil rivers, burros and camels, candy canes, miniature boats
on mirror lakes, ceramic owls and mushrooms, papier mache kings
and shepherds collected on family visits in Mexico,
trips to Disneyland and San Diego, scarlet butterflies,
tinsel waterfalls, splendid tableaux that shine
generation after generation offering shelter to the Divine.

From one neighbor's *nacimiento* to another
and another, all nine dark nights before Christmas,
the faithful process, some with images of Mary
and Joseph, some with candles,
until each one is weary, shivering, shaken,
knocking door to door

until every way they trudge
becomes the way.
Finally, there is room, here
la posada, shelter, and perhaps
rest.

~~

All through the summer I check the Buena Vista—
trellis of roses and morning glories,
hydrangea, corn and sunflowers flourish,
a new story, each in its season,
and languish.
I drive on, scanning the sky
for monarchs or song birds' migration.

December bites deep, bitter.
Bare, barren, the strip lawn extends
the length of the stucco apartment building.

This year not one flamingo,
no Lady, no one lining a tiny manger with straw.

Hope, it would appear, has moved on,
but the men who gather by the convenience store each morning
still wait for work.

BACK HOME

in the narrow border between the back porch and his half-acre garden,
    my father's seven-tree orchard—two apple, one pear, a peach,
two sweet cherry, a plum—lollygagged. Then strawberries. Gooseberry
    bushes rambled along the line between the neighbors' side yard,
their trash barrel and clothes line, and ours. My father

nursed those seven trees, called us out to see their blossoming,
    and gathered what birds or bugs overlooked for jelly or pie.
"Only two kinds of pie," he'd say, "Hot and cold. I like both." Only memory
    (the new owner's satellite dish planted in concrete): his home town,
mine too, isn't there any more either, except in reverie

as I pass the Buena Vista's corn or *nacimientos,* and swim
    mornings in the narrow lane. Uprooted farmers—*los hombros,*
my father, even me with five dwarf fothergilla and trellis—
    hunger in the diaspora of the new twenty-first century.
For years after I left home, I would hear his voice, "You'll see,

it will be all right." Now I hear, "You can do it, honey. Can't you see
    I'm dead?" So I bring all I can bear to the melangerie,
assemble and rearrange what I can't let go, apple pie, peach.
    Some days it's a sufficiency, some not. Those days I garden,
pull weeds, plant seeds, listen until I see seven blossoming trees.

LA PROMESA

Our Lady of Perpetual Hope has returned to her shrine
in the yard behind Angel's house.

In her place by the creche, school children join the attending host
of lawn sculptures, three ducks, one bunny, spotted fawn,
flamingo and swan,
                              but where are the sheep and camels kneeling

in humble veneration? And Joseph, where is he?
Usually there are shepherds near the stable, and goats.

Here, in a candlelit nave, shepherds wait,
a little restless, their plaster flock never wandering far.
From the straw-lined manger, Maria's baby cousin
waves his arms, laughing at the flamingo and camels.
Hushing the child, the young girl looks for José who's looking for the Magi
who cannot arrive until the star hangs brightly above *La Natividad.*

At last they stand on their marks, perfect, leaning on staffs, bearing gold
and myrrh, angels and their parents rejoicing. What animates the pageant—

not so much the wise man pulling at the burro's lead nor the wise man pushing
from behind, not statuary mingled with Carmelita's goats and kids—

                                                      that breathless moment
before the star bursts, before shepherds and virgin scramble for the sweetness
they were promised, *las abuelitas* smiling in memory and hope, *la memoria,*
la esperanza, la promesa de las dulces.

OLD SCARS LOOSEN   SWIMMING LAPS

How's that for a metaphor? I call
to the young woman guarding my life,
young enough to be my daughter,
the one who would have been born
each year in May.   "See," I call
(interrupting reverie of breathe-pull-glide),
  "Annie, see
I can almost turn my head enough to look back
over my shoulder." The thick bands, proud flesh
across the ribs   give way   and the numb ridges
curving along my scaffold-spine—
those old scars—loosen.

More pliant after year after year of laps upon laps,
no need to trust the rear view mirror's
reflection of depth, supple-tough,
I can look back on my own.

"Lookin' good," she calls,
young enough to be the daughter
who slipped from me   rushing red
"Push," Annie coaches. "Push
yourself but not so much you pull something.
What's the rush?"

Time, Annie, I don't have so much of,
and my daughter would not be
a blonde jock anyway, striding along the deep end,
flip flopping around the locker room, mop in hand.
Her name, we planned, would be the way
our house sits back from the road,
  modest, welcoming,
    but once inside,

spacious rooms and time enough
by open windows, border garden, blossoming beds,
light, shade, laughter and murmuring,
my daughter would be room and time.

That was the plan. If you live long enough for old scars to loosen,
you know metaphors have a way of leaving home.
Titanium rods, surgically screwed to my torque-skewed spine,
become, x-rayed, some wild game of chutes and ladders,

or the lines connecting far-flung stars
in a picture book of myths.

What doesn't show on film is what adheres,
but now they're loosening

  adhesions giving way and

        a lifetime from
     my daughter
              Annie Annie

guardian of mothers, room and time,

what holds us   if not our scars

BUENA VISTA MORNINGS

You may not always make it in time, but you always on the way.
That's all we can ask for, darling child.   —*Walter Mosley*

On the way to swim laps, I notice bedraggled sunflowers,
stalks bowed, raggedy, five or six listing toward
no pets allowed and *no standing anytime.*
Summer at half mast, they flinch
waiting for October's first patchy frost.

Do I proffer my own seasonal dread
to their shriveled leaves dangling? Empty mittens
strung through jacket sleeves, they witness mothers
fending off loss and helplessness.   Or daughters
in exile, their garments rent, *k'ria k'ria,*
   Father, I shall not forget.
Or a serried row of sisters.
Too much for sunflowers to bear,
all this significance.

Every day passing the Buena Vista, I see what the day brings,
today wind-rattled stalks for my family's *succah*—
temporary dwelling constructed each year
so stars shine through what shelters us,
eating and sleeping, a reminder
wandering is our birthright,
harvest a blessing, given or withheld.

These same stars give Inuit other songs, other games.
Far from the Buena Vista as a *succah*
from Guadalupe, stars are more than night glistening
as day glitters snow, and not sky pictures Inuit journey by.
Stars are openings where beloved dead signal
they are happy. Beyond the pierced shade

they say there is light,
fathomless   infinite,
and here   53 words for snow.

One time our firstborn told me, "Infinity goes on and on,
Momma, and more stars than you can count."
Soon he will leave our house as he left my body,
necessarily, irrevocably.
When Jacob sleeps under our roof again,
he will sojourn, a beloved guest,
as we are visitors in time.

Buena Vista mornings I find what the day offers,
    swans and hydrangeas, angels fooling
up and down a trellis, sunflowers back and forth,

    tell what my arms and legs rouse in the cool water

well loved body   diaspora daughter

    more stars than I can count

    luminous dark

Body Braille

CONTINUING EDUCATION

Kindergarten was optional.
Mother kept me home
to keep my little sister company.
Sissy napped and I looked at things—ladybugs
climbing stalks, shade inching from the Chinese elm
across our yard to the sticker bushes.
We lived at the edge of town.
Fire trucks wouldn't race past our side of the street.

First grade I sat by Jack Smith
whose mother, pretty but frowning,
came each time his nose bled.
In straight rows, we learned to color in the lines,
to print neatly, upper and lower case.

Summers we wandered, finding where State Fair Florist
dumped day-old flowers, carried lilacs by the armful,
iris, dahlias, roses and roses to Helen, soft brown Helen,
who cleaned and cared for us. We ran wild,
becoming horses
with diamond-studded hooves.

By third grade I, a blue bird reader, knew all I needed.
Then this girl, Marcy Cuffin, slow and dirty,
a different kind of dirty than farm kids, Marcy
came to sit two rows back, out of alphabet.
Her voice, when she spoke,
came from the back of her throat.
She wore a green plaid dress, too short and tight,
or a yellow print which fit ok, red sweater,
socks slumped around scabby ankles and unched
into the heels of scuffed shoes,

dark hair chopped at crazy angles,
glasses taped together.
She had this sister—Charlotte
a year behind.

They lived in that part of town
Colored wouldn't live—Lonsdale,
which leaned from the tracks as if the trains
rushing by their tarpaper walls made them shy away.

Once in gym class I couldn't help it, in a circle game
I had to take her hand.
Her palm felt dry and warm, like Joyce or Sylvia's.
Like mine, there was strength in her grip.

THE ONE STORY WE TELL

When I finally locate Mother
among the old folks in the day room,
all soft in their chairs, when I stand over her,
mouth puckered and sunk,
bosom sprawled in her own lap, I kneel before her
and touch her arm. She brings her dull
her listing gaze to mine. At last, I thought,
almost falling where I crouch,
here you are, helpless,
harmless.

Smack, smack to kingdom come, rattle
those three teeth in their gourd, spit
her maiming words back: no sport,
no sport in that. Besides,
I wrote that poem already, years before I knew
life would have its way with me, too.

Most of us have one story we tell. Oh, we might shine
its shoes, buy a snazzy book bag, new crayons,
but when you flip through the album, the same face
grins from the white grid, hopeful, more or less.

What I want is for someone to snatch me from the flames,
beat out the fire. When she holds me and I whimper
it hurts she murmurs *I know, baby, I know.*

Someone did that once for me.
Helen held me with her singed brown hands
fifty years and more. Last Friday she died,
about 7 p.m. Her sister called to say
Helen wearied, that's all,

looked around—*here*
is a good enough place. This is far enough.

Though the fire's ash and scars fade
my mother still knows who I am.
Look how she smiles.

THE HELEN POEMS

Wind chill factor nears zero.
My throat is raw. Milk warmed with honey
comforts and the memory of you
not rushing me
to drink it down fast.

My mother's surrogate general, your duty
meant enforcing her rules,
but you hadn't the heart,
let me off the hook warning,
"Why do you do like that, honey?
You know it just makes your momma wild."
One time, though, you didn't cover for me.
She found you crying *(Spit in my face.)*
 and hauled me out
to know the reason why. I spat
because children know about power,
cried because you were sobbing.

Maybe that's what being black means
in a small Missouri town in the 50's,
that and having to drive all the way
to Cole Camp for a dentist
who'd drill your teeth.
I'm guessing, Helen,
by what your mother had to leave you,
two dime store hankies you cut in fourths
to trim an organdy apron
to serve my mother's dinner guests,
rosy scallops along the white starched hem
over your pressed black dress,
bending with the silver trays,

"Thank you, Helen.
You may serve the coffee now."

I never knew your mother's name
nor saw her when we drove you home,
across the KATY tracks by the shoe factory.

She moved slow, tender, I know
by the way you let me hang on your skirt
while you ironed, sang and ironed.

If Mother and Daddy weren't there
you and I ate together, side by side

in the kitchen nook near the hot water tank.
It was warm. You were pretty.

More yielding than Mother, you sang
the long afternoons.   I pretended to color,
then later, to read.
Songs drifting on summer's heat from another room,
some without words, scared me
you might not come back on Monday,
might not return from Blueberry Hill
or wherever you and Earl went.
Then you left him,
drove away with someone else.
What came together in my grief—
sex meant losing love.
Cross my legs and hope to die
for years after. Got lucky one night
in St. Louis, Helen, I loved a man sweet
and calm as you.
My body took me from there.

One time I asked had I been bad as a child.
I wouldn't say that, your voice soothed
over the years, honey from the rock.
Same old question no matter the words.

THE HELEN POEMS ~ 2

I'm a sucker for black women of a certain age
and heft. Because of you
I expect they will care for me,
hum while they iron,
beat out fire racing up my leg, with bare hands.

Imprinted on you, I was ready to be lulled
by Sweet Honey in the Rock, leaned toward the lead singer
reaching down for the notes, her momma finding a way
when there was no way, though she's darker than you
or my memory of you, I was ready.
She's the age you were back then,

the age I am now, but still I thought she'd rock me.
Hadn't you scolded last time I called?
So what did she mean by saying
after the song about her momma
that the difference between white women and black is black

women don't have the problem of wondering
how much can they do? I wondered does she hate
those of us who can pass through white
(men) and do you, Helen,
or is it just me hating
that part of myself with the problem of knowing
I can assume an Anglo-Saxon name?

Is the part of me wanting to be rocked
the same part that might have the name fixed
the same part still asking you to clean up?

The one who goes on wanting to be rocked
goes on despite wanting.

THE HELEN POEMS ~ 3

Last night in a dream I truly was your child,
brown eyes   black braids   brown skin   small.

I stood eyeing the white man's white shirt
over his fat ole belly.
I would have gone around him
but there was only one way.

My sons paw through the heirloom dresser,
solid honey maple, spill my treasures
from the little drawer meant for collar stays and gloves—

all the this and that I mean some day
to glue in the wooden box, five sections,
in which Sarah sent me teacups from Japan,

an assemblage like Jos. Cornell and more so,
glued outside and on top, organic, inspired
by my younger son's sculptural collages.

Burrowing, my boys hold up the silver disc
from a necklace Quinn sent from Iran,
yellow feathers from a warbler, a wishbone pin,

Mother's Jewish Book of Days with an outdated *yahrzeit* list
in her cryptic script. "What's this," they demand,
taking apart my love of useless things.

"From Helen," I explain. "Part of the present she gave me
on Aunt Dee's confirmation. Knowing me,
Helen could anticipate my jealousy."

They understand and I remember
unwrapping a small zipper bag of soft quilted cotton,
Provence print, burgundy and yellow

(By then Helen no longer cleaned white women's homes.
She managed Domestications, a well-appointed gift shop
on the Plaza in K.C.),

and stuffed in the corner, a hard lump rolled
in white tissue, a ceramic box, inscribed *"Je t'aime
adjourd'hui plus qu'hier mais moins qui demain"* on the lid.

The quilted bag frayed along the zipper.
The hinges of the box gave out.
The lid I keep in my keeping drawer

for these moments with my sons
or late at night when my husband sleeps
and I walk room to room through the house.

So much happens year by year,
when I call, late December, on your birthday.
How can it be, you marveled
the year you turned fifty-eight,
the year I would turn forty.

Once you called out of a starless night,
mid-November. Should you marry
a certain gentleman who is so kind?
It had been some years since you woke
to find Charles dead beside you.
Now his daughter's moving to Seattle
with her babies, and what do I think.

Last August I called—Mother to be released
from the hospital, would you come
for a week to help her and Daddy,
it would make us all feel better having you there.
Oh child, your knee, your eyes, your own sister's health.

Hanging up, I talked over arrangements with my sister.
Everything settled, I asked if she remembered, being older,

where we stayed during Poppa Jake's funeral,
with Miss White or Mrs. Kirkman.
Sister asked do I remember when she told me
to spit at Helen.
"Why?" "So I wouldn't get in trouble."
was all she could say.

Sisters can tell you about your life,
things no one else can know—
saving things—and it happens over coffee
when you're making arrangements.

She told me to spit at Helen.
We stayed at Miss White's.

My father died. Mother's brain is strangling her mind,
disease clamping her synapses one by one
and fistsful all at once. Still she knows you, Helen,
each brown gentle aide by your name,
or as my sister says, "She'd know you in the dark."

Last night your voice quivered on the line. Would I mind
sending more fruit? Just released from hospital
only citrus tasted good.

I croon a sort of lullaby, one by one the songs
I sang my father, some without words,
calling you back from Blueberry Hill.

You girls better listen to me now.
You can't wait. Once a house is empty, word gets around.
By the time you make up your minds to gather and sort through
all your parents left, someone will beat you there
and help himself And don't you look down your noses

at those paintings either, silver, the crystal and linens, the lamps
your Grandma Deb bought in Italy. 'I don't live that way, Helen.'
What does that mean? You put them by, you keep them.
You don't know—your boys will marry and want them.
That's your heritage. You were brought up with all that.
Don't tell me another thing about it.

The obits, when all is said and done, how we'll find out
though we asked Oscar and her sister 'Ginia
to call if we could help, just let us know.
At last the circle they draw around Helen
will draw the line. Nothing I can do but wait
for the dog to bark when the paper hits the pavement,
too late too late,

what I heard that time a doe leaped into the road and there was no way
to stop, how I felt opening the car door to go look at what I knew I'd find.

So weak when I called, she asked me to write instead, asking
her way of telling what I am to do, am to do—
then I can read it over whenever I want.

Oscar died, a heart attack, lucky, before the cancer
gnawed him through.
I can't speak of him yet, but wanted you to know.
Talk about something else.

Spirea by the stone wall like Judge Hays' high hedge,
my boys whooping as they rise to the hoop,
feisty Greta and how she makes us laugh.

Good, and those pears, honey,
nothing else stayed down, but those pears
were real sweet.

Helen's right, the breakfront fits my dining room fine,
the one important thing she wanted each of us to have from home,
the one Grandma bought in Japan, curved glass door and beveled side panes,
ebony panels with scenes of pilgrims making their way up rocky golden ledges
to the orange pagoda where you'd expect sages would meditate. Instead
a smiling man flies a box kite over a bramble blooming, perhaps an idiom,
a reference to some legend a curator might interpret for the audio tour.

The prized breakfront from Grandma's Brush Creek apartment in Kansas City—
I can see where it stood, the far wall of her dining room,
where her elegant half-dressed body was found,
the fabulous breakfront, shipped to my mother in Sedalia
until we dispatched her possessions, arrived at my door damaged in transit.

All I could do—take the insurance money, restore what could be,
"insulting the damage" so new ebony adheres,
the gilt edge a tad wavery, hardly noticeable if you didn't know to look,
but he'll tell me, Burgess will, when he finds the right gold to even the edge.
He's asking around, has it posted on restoration.com.

And her painting of a Dutch interior seems to widen my dining room wall.
In the corner of my dining room broken china lies stacked,
Mother's trousseau shabbily packed,
deep-white encircled by a 22-karat band, porcelain so fine
your hand's dense shade waves when you hold a plate to the light.

Some day I'll make a sequence from the four least damaged plates,
(re)constructing my mother's passage from the lawn in Omaha,
a girl between her brothers, swimsuits wet from the sprinkler;
through courtship and young motherhood to her civic duty phase,
and the last plate—her dementia days, assemblage of all the other
broken plates in high relief.   I need the right glue

for that bricolage, strong and translucent all at once, and then what,
what will it mean I kept everything, damaged and intact, made something else
of all those broken pieces if I can't tell Helen and she doesn't say, *"I know,
baby, I know."*

A FEW WORDS ON WHAT HAPPENED

(lucky/new/body/routine/iron/other stuff/old/lucky)

Below my right knee, that hairless patch gleams—
playing too close to the flame. Lucky for me
my overalls were new, sizing not washed out,
lucky Helen looked out the kitchen window
and ran to bare-hand that fire.

No scar on the left foot unless
you count the way that foot turns in
when I'm tired, the body's memory
of childhood's shape.

Where tonsils grew there's probably a scar.
Discount it, routine procedure, if you want,
and those unwise teeth.
I say a body takes in what happens
and routine happens to someone else.

Right palm, below the thumb, that white zag
across the fleshy part won't tell anyone's life,
or love. Dark stumble, rocky path, blinded
by some grief or grievance lost to newer ones,
realia in body-Braille.

Folded between belly and a smaller mound of flesh,
scar upon scar testify to a womb called "iron,"
defied nature and pitocin,
would not willingly release those boys.

Curving from left armpit to pelvis,
trace of the rib surgeons sawed off
to loosen vertebrae which curved a helix all their own.

Pearlously from neck to sacroiliac, scar upon scar
wends along that willy-nilly backbone, fused,
with rib stuff and other stuff.

These are the ones that show. I only mention them
because today an old friend stopped me—
his ailments alphabetized, specialists catalogued, ISBN's
for every supplement, capsule, and balm.

Promise that won't be us. When we're old
as his old, a couple rocking on some porch,
these scars of mine will bore us both.

Unless I'm lucky
and you still trace them, tender, loving
all my body tells
about what happened.

OPEN WINDOW

The woman who chose to do without her other breast
does not fear cancer recurring so much
as she's grown tired of references to Amazons,
their bowstrings whirring unimpeded, arrows flying undeflected to their mark,
tired of being cajoled into courage.
    Besides, her one breast felt lonely lopsided silly.
She prefers how the surgeons froze her nipples and reattached them
on the smooth slight mounds of scar.

She remembers her younger body,
the glee when her mother finally said ok
she could sleep at the foot of the bed, her head
under the open window, wear only the bottoms
of seersucker 'jams. That's how she knew summer
was really here.
                She can just hear the refrain
"*. . . on Blueberry Hill,*"
                   the screen door bang
as Helen leaves for the day,
and the bedtime sky isn't all the way dark.
She can make out the swing set, clothes line, their garden—
rounded shapes of darkness she knows are tomatoes, kale, beets.

She wants to sleep that way tonight,
promising dreams, a light breeze playing
over her almost androgynous chest.
She wants her younger sister in the twin bed, their older sister
down the hall, grown-up voices drifting through the deepening night,
the dog sighing as she settles under the window. Sugar
we named the caramel-colored stray, "Sugar, here girl."

46

COMING TO REST

If you're lucky enough and live
long enough you may understand

then, only then, only now—
the whole story, what you left unsaid,

amending what you could know then,
become willing to tell the rest.

That day in the nursing home my mother
saw me, her face becoming the sun, moon

and stars so happy was she to see me.
I met her gaze and averted my eyes.

⁓⁓

Now I know where we sat was its own kind
of holy place. I could have held her gaze,

my fingertips to hers, creating a new world
for us, but asked, "Why now—when it's too late?"

Time is a funny business, expanding, contracting,
tzim tzummm, swallowing the years,

the days' own tail, rolling on minute by minute,
reinventing seconds and nanoseconds,

dark years, and light, dark   light   evening
coming back to *there* and *then*: Oak Grove,

⁓⁓

ten miles from Blue Springs by way of Grain Valley,
Missouri Route 7. No telling what could have been

had we clothed ourselves as lamb and lion (who
was she? was I?), if we had laid down our swords,

our shields, taken up pruning hooks against
the spent, superfluous brambles, that hedge

of sticker bushes between us, if I, too,
that day had been willing. My mother smiled,

clothing me in garments of light—raiment, her delight
in me, not minding all we lived through together.

~ ~

There now, I have told the rest. And you have read these words.

~ ~

Now let her be wherever death takes our loved ones.
Now let her memory float gently, a leaf on living water.

Tashlich, burdens of years past tossed on the river—how light
we feel casting them off, watching them move on, out of sight.

Remember the little boats sent downstream at Scout camp,
candlelit to mark their passage, each bearing into darkness

a child's best hope? Or the paper lanterns Buddhists light
and set afloat to honor those who lived, and left us here,

comforting their souls, and ours, extinguished by the water,
indistinguishable from the river. How can there be *too late?*

Palimpsest

"On my desk there is a stone
with the word 'Amen' carved on it."
— Yehuda Amichai

PALIMPSEST: FEZ
for Ellen

For every teaching there is a language,
to give our stories a body and breath.
And for every absence there is a name.

In Fez we wandered out from the market,
the bartering, strong smells of spice and fish,
up and down narrow streets to find where

our guide told us Jews once lived. He pointed
toward what had been the Jewish graveyard,
headstones crushed to pave new neighborhoods.

Synagogue now home to a post office,
the Talmud Torah used for cinema,
quiet until the matinee at 2:00.

No Jews in Fez, not a sign, except doorposts,
faint traces where *mezzuzot* had been nailed,
their absence all that remains.

GOING BACK IN TIME

Normal means chicken soup simmering to ward off cold, adding more salt.
Normal is griping about deer in the tulips, phoning a husband to bring home milk,
figuring out e-mail.

Sitting on the hearth, cool slate, scissors, stout twine, I return to normal,
sorting paper to recycle, newspapers in one pile, slick coated stock in another,
magazines and catalogues—normal—a sale on back-to-school supplies.

Front page headlines: TERROR ASSETS FROZEN, AIRSPACE AND ARMS OFFERED BY RUSSIANS
(How *Times* have changed, just a little joke, business almost as usual.), then
Monday's, Sunday's, Saturday's, Friday's UNLESS AFGHANISTAN SURRENDERS

BIN LADEN NOW, Thursday's 1000S PRESUMED DEAD, Wednesday's U.S. ATTACKED
HIJACKED JETS DESTROY, back to Tuesday, September 11, 2001, early edition,
when tough primary elections and Michael Jordan's basketball return were news.

Normal is checking homework. Normal is even a friend dying of AIDS. Normal
is making my way through Days of Awe, ten of them, aiming for Yom Kippur
when I go up to recount the ancient Temple Service of the High Priest.

Back then normal was a special chamber where elders read him LEVITICUS,
changing his linen garments five times, five ritual immersions, vestments of gold,
slaughtering bullocks. Normal was confessing sins,

designating one goat "for Azazel," one "for the Lord,"
scarves waved signal post to post from Jerusalem to the wilderness and back,
a year of blessing, corn and wine and oil, a year of rejoicing in our land, fully blessed.

And the High Priest's final prayer, *For the inhabitants of Sharon, who live in peril
of sudden earthquakes, May it be Your Will, our God and God of our fathers,
that their homes not become their graves.*

LITTLE SISTER

Helping her husband die
is any journey.
You offer water,
share what your pockets hold,
sing.

But your sister—
her death you take
into your arms
and wrestle,
into your own body,
a knife between the ribs,
love between your legs
until you grow big with it.

Just the possibility fills you,
rounds your belly.
You pant for breath.
Squatting and grunting
you bring forth your future
and death is no longer someone else's.
Death is something you hold in your arms,
croon and give suck to.
Generations make sense now,
the need for them.
There is room in your body
for this knowing.

Little sister, little sister death.

DAYS OF AWE

after Yehuda Amichai

After Amichai read, slips of gold paper
marking his poems
flew out from the book, rose
      as messages to *HaMakom*
         in the balance

of paper and air.
After Amichai read, sparks
flew out from the book
     touch us   touch us
and the souls of the letters
hovered.
  Between earth and sky
   rose the words
      beloved dead
and they guttered around his feet.

And so gold
fluttering
settled
marking the place he would turn toward,
malachi's golden feathers,
so much wrestling,
one way of being
held.

"AFTER LIFE"

a film by Hirokazu Kore-eda,
the story of people selecting a single memory-feeling to take into eternity

The four of us sit around the dining room table,
Saturday evening. Soon Jacob and Owen
will be read to sleep. Right now Owen's brother
and parents are teaching him UNO, rules
that don't dance to Jacob's fiddling, more confusing
than the rules.
                    Owen begins to understand the sequence
of play. Triumphant, he plays green three on my red two.
Triumphant, Jacob yells, "No! red or two!"
                                    Cards pile up round
by round. (At some point corn is popped and buttered. By spring
a black dog will live here too.)
                                Owen offers his yellow nine
for my blue eight. Jacob will correct him, savagely this time, and
their dad holds up his palm broad as a crossing guard's,
says gently, "Owen is a special case."
                                    Jacob gets it. I can see
he understands his brother has learned all he can for one night.
Almost seven, Jacob holds back, a giant leap.
                                    Owen gets it too,
no punching or kicks. Momma won't be pulling brother off him rolled
into a ball the way caterpillars roll. Owen plays his golden nine, sing-
songing, "I'm a special case," smiling, "a special case."
Daddy plays yellow. So do Jacob and I; then Owen plays green
or blue, red and yellow until our evening ends.

This feeling I could live on forever, so long as *this*
includes knowing I chose the moment, the table, cards shuffled
and dealt while dark-cold circles our house, savoring all this
in so many words.   Maybe after life,
feeling would be enough, knowing not so vital,
just let's wait and see.

RAPTOR

Before the boy sat in my kitchen
rapture meant more about birds of prey
than prayer, some aural, feral association
between sighting the merest twitch or rustling,
aiming your whole self and letting fly.

Seated at the table,
held blissful by the winter night,
the scent of onions stirred in olive oil,
wrapped in poems wrought from stone and blossoms
changing how we see and hear,

poems and their music rearranging the cells in our brains,
the tiny bursts of fire synapse to synapse, what we think,
maybe why we think, having the words to shape desire.

Dumbstruck
Spellbound
Rapt

Only once before did I witness
a face so shining, enraptured,
my husband
returning from the *mikvah,*
newly blessed, renamed,
light extending the shape of his body—

Moses descending Sinai,
ten Words igniting a crown
Michaelangelo mistook for horns.

There's no mistaking rapture,
a man transformed
by water and the *kavanah* of certain speech.

Speechless I drew him to me,
embracing what burned but did not consume,
our sons whooping and dancing
around us, coming only
so close

⁓ ⁓

And what of the prey?
After generations of death
grew camouflage, buff, dun,
grey, ruddy brown, colors of prairie grass
in winter, no leaves or brush to hide in,
betrayed by her own breath or hunger,
safe so long as she held still,
or stirring, close to her burrow.

What if she strayed into the bird's eye view?
What did she call the riveting talons,
the natural order, awe and ecstasy?

⁓ ⁓

The snap of oil, singe of onion and garlic
in cast iron brought me back
to the stove, shaken and grateful
for salt and the need to stir.
I talked some more
and still
not hearing a sound from the boy,
for want of anything else,

I recited some lines to draw him
back along the line of his soul,
back into his own body,
flannel shirt, corduroy trousers
brick red, gold.

ISAAC'S SON

No one should go on dying like that.
So you held him. Isaac's son, or Jacob's,
you cradled his feet,
your cheek against his knees,
as his wife held his body to her body's
fierce warmth.
                    Mortal friend,
retrieve your father's *tallis* from the mourning bench.
Wrap it around your cello before you close the case.

Let all you love fill that rich silence.

Hold the music in your arms.

PALIMPSESTINA: THE DAY ROOM

Not intimate while she was our Mother,
when she became our Child, Affection came.
Her gaze, when her wandering eyes find me,
grows spacious and warm, even luminous.
My own eyes brim but still I do not reach
for her, soft and pink, fearing a sudden

return to speech. She might regret her sudden
welcome and rake me with hot words. Mother,
helpless not harmless, her fathomless reach
sends me sprawling again where no help came.
From the far corners light draws in. Luminous
island, day room table she shares with me.

The other patients, blurring, fade, and me
a fawn stunned in her headlights. A sudden
clang, ward doors burst open, voluminous
smells from aluminum cart. "Lunch, Mother."
Applesauce, broth, pureed meat—how she came
to this sodden mess resembling phlegm and reach

could be traced easily enough. I reach
for her spoon. She smiles, her gaze disarms me.
Wordless thoughtless helpless love overcame
all fear, and now my hands, in their sudden
rise. Why not when love could matter, Mother,
why now, this room? while time, this loom in us,

weaves, unravels and weaves the luminous
shroud? binds and unbinds the swaddling reach
of memory? Not she, but I the mother,
not she—my infant son, nursing, holds me
in his deep blue gaze, draws me in. Sudden
warmth, milk letting down, oh there there love came.

Momma. Now, her eyes dimming, she became
my child. Merciful words, illumine us
who speak in half light and glare of sudden
knowing. Broth dribbles from her lips. I reach
for soft napkins, as many before me,
to blot the names, my daughter, my mother.

Where she and I came my son and I'll reach,
my blue eyes luminous when he feeds me.
A man suddenly with child to mother.

EARLY MORNING WALK: SUN AND MOON

Tart September air opens the day,
otherwise, walking the familiar road
past the same houses, past the same subtle variations
of butterfly bush and vines,

I might have somehow missed the balancing sky,
pale moon setting over my western shoulder,
pale sun rising over the east

and I can almost see the wire joining them,
the moon and the sun, the setting and rising,
to walk on, evening to dawn

and the paved road becomes a path
through this moment,
a ladder like Jacob's,
a way

～ ～

Another morning emblem
earlier in the year, March,
earlier in the day so the sky is wholly black.
Fear and pain crunch the gravel
as we rush our firstborn for surgery
and Look! my son points directly ahead and up,

the old moon, the morning star almost in her arms,
suspended precisely between her palms

tossing him up, laughter   laughter
or reaching out for him, *here, water*

a prayer like Hagar's
a way for

my lost sister
to reach me.

REHABLEAUX

Flickering down the midnight hall
wardens
in the out and out battle with pain

surround the crib next to mine
where a woman clutches the rails.
Circling the curtain
they become shadow
puppets, a Balinese tableau.
                              Archipelago
    of bent straws,
                    thin coverlets.
She wants her mother.
They give what they can, respite
in the fray of nerve and knitting bone,

each one lying alone in her body
in her narrow bed.

Mine banks a window, dark panes refracting night,
by day framing uncommon blue
and, below roof line,
            a rocking scaffold,   two men repointing bricks,
    their safety harness swinging, clamped to the rail.

Unleashed by morphine I float

        beyond railing, through wanting

all that holds me
                    over the mineshaft,
          plummeting after a yellow song-
bird,
          flicker
 flutter   a cotillion of moths
around me,
              aflame

THE BEACHCOMBER'S ART

Once after a storm on Okracoke Island
the menfolk walked the beach.
Sun dazzled the water,
sand reflected the sea's glitter.
They watched tiny crabs tunnel in sand,
watched pipers dance with waves.
They brought back shells and fragments of shells
in fantastic shapes, each with its own story
that began "in a faraway place called home."

They brought back shells and mermaids' purse
and the bones of a whale, yes, the bones of a whale
picked from the skeleton gleaming clean
from tides and storm, the gulls and sun,
rib bones, lithe and curved as flutes should be.
I wish I had gone with them, I would know
what to make of it, now, I would get it right,
cord and whale's rib, some feathers and shells,
maybe then when we hung the amulet
the wind would sing in the bones.

PALIMPSEST: GIRL AT THE WINDOW

A small girl standing on a low bench leans against her mother seated there.
A girl, her flannel nighty flared with warm air from the furnace vent,
leans on her mother gazing out the window. Snow drifts. Evening drifts.
Leans into her mother whose left arm encircles her daughter's waist.
No one emerges from the swirling darkness to make his way to them,
not a husband or father, not neighbor or friend, because this painting

is not about coming home or even being home. Snow, wait! the window
is the frame is the girl's home. She borrowed someone else's memory
to be there. In a minute the scene will change. The woman, after all,
will tire of this weight on her, will find some pretext to move away,
ringing phone, boiling pot. The girl will find herself watching snow swirl
beneath the night sky's dome. Leaning against the window frame,

her forehead rests on cool glass. For all I know she is still looking out,
but of course, she isn't. When she understands no one is coming,
she slides off the bench to look for her mother talking on the phone,
in the kitchen stirring. It took a long time to know that no one will come,
mother won't return, so she is hungry, wants the macaroni. She wants more,
won't ask. She is busy making up her childhood. Girl. Window. Home.

ABOVE PASTURE LOOP

What if it's true you can't move on
until the town inside you dies?
What if home is no longer where you live?

Across pasture grown back to meadow,
through old growth forest,
up Barring Hill he'd climb
every afternoon,

murmuring as the sun set,
 not the German he taught beginners,
tracing declensions down the blackboard,
coupling modifiers behind nouns,
 not Goethe, nor Schiller
from his wait-listed seminars.

For the ones left at home, already memory
when he fled over the Alps, and for the dead,
he set out homely words for stones.
What he said, watching garnet-gold
brush with darker light, who can rightly say,
but to the stand of birch and fir
his students brought an alabaster bench
engraved with his name.

Happenstance is the rise above pasture loop.
Still day after day drifts to twilight. Home lies close
to where you find yourself and climb there once a day.

EARLY MORNING, MOUNTAIN AND DEER

This morning when I walk along the river,
a mountain the Dutch named the Hook
softens along the pearl gray sky. The crags become a woman
drowsing, her hip round as the firmament,
head pillowed on her shoulder.
Her arm reaches the growing light. *Good morning, mother.*

For a step my eyes tear, a certain kind of prayer. I only hear the deer,
two of them, cross the road, slipping from the woods
to browse in the meadow.
                    Somewhere in the near distance, toward the river
a hound rejoices. The doe leaps back across the road to the still black trees
where her fawn lies hidden.
                    Oh the mothers who resemble mountains,
the daughters camouflaged in dark morning leaves.

MORNING MINYAN

Seven I count by the morning star's light,
      deer crossing from meadow to woods.

On the meadow side of the road,
      flicker of shade upon darkness,
two more caught by my lamp.

They wait for me to retreat
      three prayer steps,
and join the rest in the hollow
      blackberry fills with winter brambles.

Or,
in the hollow blackberry fills with winter
      they wait for me

ROMARE BEARDEN IN MECKLENBERG

"Autumn Lamp" and "November—Cherokee Lands"
paintings with collage

This is what life is for,
silver lamp on a glowing plank,
Uncle Aubrey's shoulders rising orange
out of the blues, dark rosiny hands laid over his lap.
Romare remembers leaning against his uncle's thigh,
listening to the hum after the tune was sung,
the warm place where their bodies
held on to the song. Momma's big brother.
For that faraway boy at the man's side
he paints *guitar*, strung golden, cat gut his whole length,
form and throat to the tuning pegs.
He paints himself there below Aubrey's heart.

Romare, a dreamy child, can stare at nothing
longer   than anything   in particular
he favors light on leaves, nothing brighter or quicker.
Romare saves the doe he faced on the evening
path, takes her to the small chamber
where they continue gravely
to regard each other,
(Oh her elegance and black-tipped ears.)
Romare steps aside to watch her
pass him on the woodsy path

He cuts her dark eyes out
of paper sleek as the night sky,
glues her night eyes on clean canvas
and paints her face around them
delicate and wild
Somewhere her fawn waits
so he paints *fawn* among leaves

He remembers the line along the backbone
and the spots of light. He pastes undergrowth
to hide the creature. Romare steps back
to wait for the doe gladdened
by his brush and more so by the pattern
of stones and trees and clouds.
How the eye follows them away
to the new moon
and stars.

THE PALIMPSALMIST'S LAMENT

Who will employ biographers when history blogs down?
E-mail corresponds to whom? *So sorry to learn of*
your mother's death. Wounds as if night be a blessing.
Where is the archive for these shades of meaning?
In deep cyberspace, who unearths the artifacts?
What to make of the work of our virtual hands?

MORNING, POSSUM

On the road last night the possum
lay, feet drawn up and freshly red, blood
in a staggered ribbon from the open mouth.
                              What could we say,
my son and I, what should I, on our way to evening chores?
We trained our lights along bristled fur, slender pointing tail,
teeth sharp as a saw's blade.

                         Dawn, and she still lay there,
perfect in her early morning repose. Somehow no animal
had found her yet, no tire tracked her blood.

Walking to the river I brushed past hedges all branch and twigs.
A thorn snagged my sleeve, and wind.
Light etched clouds from the darkness over the water,
and on the rise of the far hill, each tree a dark rose on its stem.
                              All morning my mind returned
to the possum. I remembered the poem about a stillborn cat,
the one eye looking back into his own marvelous body,
laid to rest in a summer field,
and the one about fox bones restored to the woods.

Crow touched down and dipped his beak into possum's mouth,
    the last sounds wrapped in her tongue.

Bending, and shy, I pulled thick gloves from my pockets,
draped burlap over and under,
carried possum where earth was opened intimately
and leaves had fallen to cover her up.
                         This story is not a book unleashing war
to free slaves. Those words come few, and far between.
    But for the kitten, the fox and the crow,

for my son and the animals we were
            on our way to feed, I carried a possum
to some willows rimming a pond, and buried her. Today,
            the year's smallest, was given to me for this and no more,
and these words to tell time by,
though the crow didn't like me much, nor the grackle.

EARLY MORNING WALK: JULIO

for BK

Lucky that day I was alone.
My fellow walker who fears big dogs
did not clutch my sleeve as this rough beast
lunged for my ankle. I spun away reaching down
for a branch, stabbing leaves
at the snarling teeth, near, near enough to see fur bristle
on the hooligan neck.
Jab. Jab. My thin sword snapped,
the cur yelped, the last jagged thrust
enough this time.

A few steps on I found a thicker stick,
struck out north, the usual route
above the river, and circled back toward home.
The breeze picked up
wands of mountain laurel.
Grasses tossed their fringe.
Dawn broke.
Luck ran out,
sank fangs
into my smooth
muscled calf.
' hacked and hacked.
It backed away
snarling slathering
to a red brick house.

What hurt more
was the woman
at the picture
window

of that house
watching
opening
her door.

I waited
for her
to step
out
ask
could she
call
home
for me.

"Julio, Julio,
here boy."
And that
was that—

how it begins, evil,
pedestrian
as a morning walk.

Sky brightens.
Day greens around me
making my way,
braced
by a thicker stick,
watching my back.

Oh Brother Elm, Mother Storm
who dropped his branch within reach,
where
is there
a stick
thick
enough?

PALIMPSEST: RATUSHINSKAYA

Irina in her gulag cell carved words,
burnt matchsticks on a bar of brown lye soap.
Bone cold, hunger stricken, she wrote, pacing
miles enough to reach Moscow and revise.
Murmuring, Irina incised each line,
each poem (two years, three) on her mind.
Eyes closed, she could see the letters
rise, shadows of inky iridescence.

Once in awhile, guards brought prisoners water.
Before Irina lathered, she traced
her chiseled words, crooning them softly.
Face, arms, thighs, breast scrubbed by graven poems.
Smooth slate in hand, the poet struck a match.
Black fire on strong soap, Irina wrote.

BIRD SANCTUARY

Patiently we crouch in the blind.
We stare out narrow rectangles for shooting
film, to document our life list.
Our yield this morning: three rabbits, two toads,
water striders, whirligig beetles with air bubbles
on their abdomens for underwater breathing,
marsh wren, grackle, bittern, yellow throats,
sora rails, but not one blue heron.

Perhaps they have already come for the season
and gone. Another sora rail, related to the augur rails
nesting south of here on the Jersey shore,
sora sora—I think of my mother's girlhood
friend, Sora Miriam, dead some fifty years,
and of my sister named for her—
and now I understand why I have waited all morning
in the airless heat of the Upper Canada Migratory Bird Sanctuary.
This poem is for my friend Sarah waiting
impatiently in Poznan for her child
to be conceived, and for her husband, the flashes of joy
in their steady purposeful coupling,

and this poem is in memory of Sarah's father
who carried her in his arms
one summer night twenty-five years ago,
woke her from dreams to witness
Paalgrin's Comet flare across the dark field.
He named the constellations and told her the truth about stars,
they are always in the sky,
moving in their slow silent paths, and this poem is in praise of the brain,
nodding on its stem, milkweed poised for silent explosions of seed,
floating dreamily from sora to Sarah,

Ontario to Poznan,
the child not yet conceived to the child in her father's arms
and the stream of light moving in its silent
steady way through our lives.

SONG FOR BREATH AND WING BONE

Wing bones are hollow for soaring by.
Mine grow porous moonrise by womb-flow,
and breath's frame honeycombs for song.

What was marrow my babies made their own,
oh another song for breath and eggbone,
sweet song of the blood-o, blood-o, another sweet
song for the rose, last of the eggsweet blood.

Had I known that blood the last-o, last-o,
I would have sung *baruch haba*, yes, and
bless their going, sweet red going-song. Bless

one who keeps on singing, she keeps singing,
another way of telling time-o, time-o,
sweet womb song for telling time,
another woman song for keeping time.

She keeps singing til her time's by, time's by,
she keeps singing for her time flies,
time flies singing time by, oh one last time

on the wing bone, honeycomb,
last sweet song on the wing bone,
red going-song of mine.

DAYBREAK, THE DOE, THE TREES

She leaped through thin air into the deep pine woods.
I lower myself where she had rested,
where the grass still holds her warmth.
Her scent hovers in the dry air.

Daybreak. I could watch the sky ripen,
that ruddy smear above the trees' dark fringe.
I could watch the river shimmer in this widening day.
I close my eyes. I give myself back

to the mornings
my sisters and I gathered at the guest room door,
twisting our nightgowns and whispering,
"Is she awake yet?" "Look, I think she's awake"
until our mother's mother lifted the brown covers,
a meadow bird's wing. We nestled there
and she covered us with her own powdery scent
like a *tallis*.

Does shelter wear another name?
Can comfort be found anywhere else

than on this hillside, drowsing, waiting
for her to return? Perhaps some other young one waits.
Perhaps in the language she speaks now she has another name,
some sound that fills the clearing with light.
Let me call her Nehama, a resting place,
for those who vanish in the trees.

EARLY MORNING CHIAROSCURO

Snowy woods   movement
among thick black trees   skunk.
Shades of gray and darker gray, she
emerges from the white ground,
her indisputable plume
eloquent in the chilled air,
glides between flakes and shadows,
leaving delicate traces.

Farther along   a raccoon,
all ragged stripes and frozen snarl,
drifts into memory under deep white cold

and my own morning prints   all but gone.

Tracing my steps home I find my place
in the woods, why I walk in the days' early hours—

to calm myself enough to remember and know,
to surprise myself walking, finding words, dark,
cold and white-hot names in the snow,

to greet skunk and raccoon
on equal terms, and love
even the snow
whiting out
our tracks

PALIMPSESTETS

Even at her funeral they want to talk about him.
All sorrows can be born if we put them in a story.
But those pears, honey, those pears were real sweet.
If we put them in a story all sorrows can be born.
Without them is the rest of my life.
All sorrows can be born if we put them in a story.

*Under this wallpaper of willow leaves and birds
is another one with loops* of small roses.
Under the yellow roses is lumber that was timber,
a stand of burr oak, maple or pine felled by an ax
that was ore deep in the earth before smelting,
ore deep in the earth before smelting.

Photographs fade to a sepia wash.
Still she tells who sat with Aunt Anna
on the front steps in Omaha, *Did you get
what you wanted?* who moved West and never wrote again,
who waltzed with Isaac and *did you get what you wanted
from this life, even so?*

My body split open. And lava flowed?
I became a trellis. With tangled vines?
My mother wrapped herself in wind?
Twice I clambered up on the silver table.
The new moon lay in the old moon's arms.
The whole point of composing is to sound inevitable.

LAST LIGHT OVER MASHOMAC

washes the bay a deeper blue.
The water casts this darker light
skyward and twilight floods
the window, a porous membrane
we wait behind. We can still see the island
where the old ones go by water.
We wait to hear another has gone,
her spirit wandering out and back to us,
calling with her pale arms.
When the day evens out like this,
only my belly, a seven-month moon,
rises above anything else.
We wait for the one
who has brought dreams back,
the small one coursing through us
who will join us with time.
Some evening we will walk
down to the sea wall,
swim out toward the line
where the light becomes black water
and the water black light,
one will call and one will watch us go.

NOTES

Definitions of most nonEnglish words are either Spanish (Sp) or Hebrew (H).

(las) **abuelitas** - (Sp) "little" grandmothers, a term of endearment

baruch haba (H) - welcome, literally "blessed are those who come"

(las) **dulces** (Sp) - sweets, candy and cakes

(la) **esperanza** (Sp) - hope

HaMakom (H) - literally "the Place," one of the names for God and idiom for gravestone

(los) **hombros** (Sp) - shoulders, i.e. manual laborers

"Je t'aime adjourd'hui plus qu'hier mais moins qui demain." (Fr) - I love you more than yesterday but less then tomorrow.

kavanah - (H) prayerful intention

k'ria (H) - ritual rending of garments as a sign of mourning

Mashomac - Shinnecock, "where they go by water"

mikvah (H) - a bath used for ritual purification

minyan (H) - quorum of 10 adult Jews needed for public worship of certain prayers and rituals such as the mourner's kaddish

Nacimientos (Sp) - Mexican tradition dating back to 16th century, homemade nativity scenes, constructed either in or outside homes. Often multi-tiered, vivid, fanciful, many reflect a love of miniatures. Decorations traditionally include waterfall made of tinsel, a tin foil river, and a cave or mountain. Figures are added yearly and *nacimientos* may be handed down generation to the next. Each *nacimiento* is a stop in *las posadas*, a Mexican and Mexican-American custom taking place the nine nights before Christmas. In emulation of Mary and Joseph who seek shelter (*posada*) before Jesus' birth, neighbors and families gather for candlelight processions, usually ending at a church. Along the way, they have parties that include breaking *pinatas* and eating *la pan dulce* and hot chocolate. Only on Christmas Eve, is baby Jesus laid in the manger.

(La) **Natividad** (Sp) - the Birth, Nativity scene   In some Mexican towns, there is a custom of mingling live animals or people and statuary in the same Nativity scene or pageant.

palimpsest - A manuscript, typically of papyrus or parchment or a clay tablet, that has been written on more than once, with the earlier writing incompletely erased and often legible.

pardes (H) - orchard, and root for the English word 'paradise'

(la) **posada** (Sp) - shelter

(la) **promesa** (Sp) - promise

succah (H) - booth or hut. A *succah* is a temporary structure built for the 8-day celebration of the holiday, *Succot*, in recognition of dwellings built by Israelites after their Exodus from Egypt when they followed Moses through the desert to Canaan, a journey of 40 years. In Jewish tradition, the structure must be at least three-sided and stars seen through the "roof" of branches. Observant Jews eat and sleep in the huts, which are constructed in backyards of homes or at synagogues and schools. Guests share meals in the *succah* and spiritual guests, such as the patriarchs or prophets, are also "invited" by reciting a special blessing.

tallis (H) - prayer shawl

tzim tzum - (H) a Kabbalist belief that God needed to constrict or contract God's own holiness to provide room for creation

(los) **vecindarios** (Sp) - neighborhoods

yahrzeit (H) - anniversary of a death

A brief note on the Jewish calendar: Because the Jewish calendar is lunar and the secular calendar is solar, events such as *yahrzeit* and holidays do not necessarily coincide. This difference between the two calendars results in Jewish holidays being "early" or "late" in a particular secular year. Seven times every 19 years a leap month is added to the Hebrew calendar to help synchronize the two, a process called intercalation.

The Hebrew day begins at sunset, corresponding to the Biblical account of creation in *Genesis*. First there was darkness and then light was created, making days and time as we understand the terms.

ACKNOWLEDGMENTS: ATTRIBUTIONS

The poem "Morning, Possum" refers to two poems by Mary Oliver, the stillborn cat to her poem "The Kitten," and the fox bones to her poem "Fox Bones Restored to the Woods."

The poem "Buena Vista Mornings" has an epigram, "You may not always make it in time, but you always on the way. That's all we can ask for, darling child." from Walter Mosley's story "Gray-eyed Death" in *Six Easy Pieces*.

The poem "Palimpsestets" quotes the work of other poets. Section 1: "All sorrows can be borne if we put them in a story." - Isek Dinesen. Section 2: "Under this wallpaper of willow leaves and birds/ . . . is another one with loops of small yellow roses." - Kate Barnes' poem, "Coming Back" in *Where the Deer Were*. Section 3: "And did you get what you wanted from this life,/even so?" -Raymond Carver, "Late Fragment." And Section 4:"The whole point of composing is to sound inevitable." is from Aaron Copeland's journal.

The first two lines of the poem "Palimpsestina: the Day Room" paraphrases a letter from Emily Dickinson to Elizabeth Holland.

ACKNOWLEDGMENTS: COLLABORATIONS

"Daybreak, the Doe, the Trees" and "Morning, Possum" have been set to music by the jazz composer and pianist, Paulette Thompson.

ACKNOWLEDGMENTS: PUBLICATIONS

Some of the poems in *Palimpsest* have been previously published. Thanks are given to the editors of these journals and anthologies for permission to reprint them. *Red Delicious* is a chapbook published by toadlily press in the anthology *Desire Path*, the inaugural volume of the Quartet Series.

"Bird Sanctuary" – *New Traditions* and *Red Delicious**
"Days of Awe" – *Natural Bridge* and *Red Delicious*
"Early Morning, Mountain and Deer" – *Rough Places Plain: Poems of the Mountains*
"The Helen Poems 1 -5 & 10" – *Connected*
"Last Light over Mashomac" – *Nimrod* and *Red Delicious*
"Morning Minyan" – *Poetry Motel* and *Red Delicious*
"Morning, Possum" – *Nimrod* and *Red Delicious*
"Old Scars Loosen Swimming Laps" – *Mom Egg*
"The One Story We Tell" – *Connected*
"Palimpsest: Fez" – *String Poet*
"Palimpsestets" – *Earth's Daughters*
"Palimpsestina" – *Mezzo Cammin* and *Red Delicious*
"Slow Water Deep Time" – *Isotope*
"Song for Breath and Wing Bone" – *Red Delicious*

ABOUT THE AUTHOR

Maxine Silverman is the author of four chapbooks: *Survival Song, Red Delicious* (in *Desire Path*, inaugural volume of the Quartet Series from Toadlily Press), *52 Ways of Looking*, and *Transport of the Aim, a garland of poems on the lives of Emily Dickinson, Thomas Wentworth Higginson and Celia Thaxter.* Winner of a Pushcart Prize, she has published poems and essays in journals (among them *Nimrod, Natural Bridge, Isotope, StringPoet, Lilith, Mezzo Cammin, Mom Egg, Heliotrope,* and *The Westchester Review*), anthologies (among them *Pushcart Prize III, Voices within the Ark, Splinters & Fragments/Earth's Daughters, WomanPoet: Midwest, Connected: What Remains as We All Change,* and *Poems to Live By*), and *Enskyment: Online Archive of American Poetry.* "Life List" has been inscribed on granite at Edmands Park in Newton, MA—her most unusual form of publication so far.

A native of Sedalia, MO, she now lives in the Hudson River valley with her husband and garden, and they're the parents of two grown sons. In addition to poetry, she creates collage, bricolage and visual midrash. Her website is www.maxinegsilverman.com.

Photo credit: Howard Andrews

Jean Syed - *Sonnets* (2009)

Madeline Tiger - *The Atheist's Prayer* (2010),
    From the Viewing Stand (2011)

James Tolan - *Red Walls* (2011)

Brian Volck - *Flesh Becomes Word* (2013)

Henry Weinfield - *The Tears of the Muses* (2005),
    Without Mythologies (2008), *A Wandering Aramaean* (2012)

Donald Wellman - *A North Atlantic Wall* (2010),
    The Cranberry Island Series (2012)

Sarah White - *The Unknowing Muse* (2014)

Anne Whitehouse - *The Refrain* (2012)

Martin Willetts Jr. - *Secrets No One Must Talk About* (2011)

Tyrone Williams - *Futures, Elections* (2004),
    Adventures of Pi (2011)

Kip Zegers - *The Poet of Schools* (2013)

www.dosmadres.com